A ROOKIE READER®

THE GREAT BUG HUNT

By Bonnie **Dobkin**

Illustrated by Tom **Dunnington**

Prepared under the direction of Robert Hillerich, Ph.D.

Children's Press®
A Division of Scholastic Inc.
New York • Toronto • London • Auckland • Sydney
Mexico City • New Delhi • Hong Kong
Danbury, Connecticut

For Kevin, the Joy-Boy

Library of Congress Cataloging-in-Publication Data

Dobkin, Bonnie.
  The Great Bug Hunt / by Bonnie Dobkin; illustrated
by Tom Dunnington.
      p.   cm. — (A Rookie reader)
  Summary: Children set out looking for insects and
they find all kinds.
    ISBN 0-516-42017-8
    [1. Insects—Fiction. 2. Stories in rhyme.]
  I. Dunnington, Tom, ill. II. Title. III. Series.
PZ8.3.D634Gr   1993
[E]—dc20   93-10333
                                                    CIP
                                                    AC

Printed in China
18 19 20 R 09 08 07   62

Grab a jar.
No time to play!
The Great Bug Hunt
begins today.

4

Bugs! All sizes,
shapes, and kinds!
Who knows how many
we will find?

Bugs with stripes,
bugs with spots,
bugs that look
like little dots.

ladybug

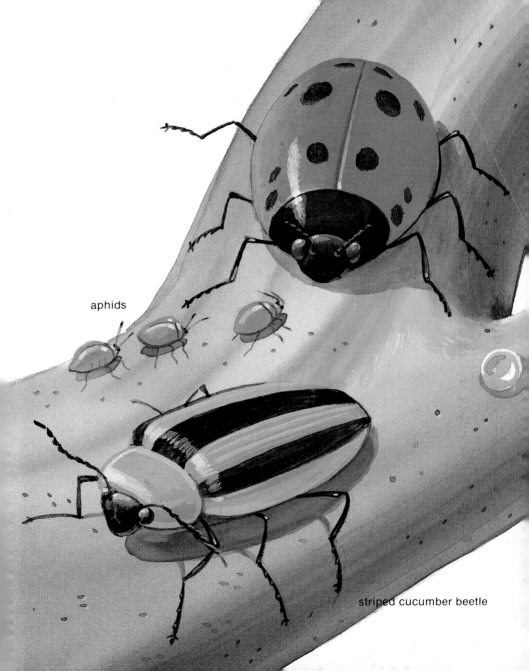

aphids

striped cucumber beetle

garden spider

dragonfly

Bugs that crawl,
bugs that fly,
bugs in cobwebs
way up high.

ant

milkweed bug

9

caterpiller

10

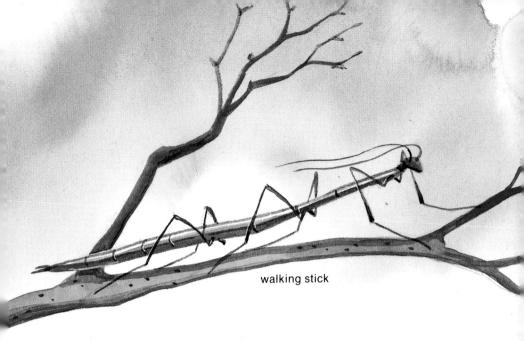
walking stick

Fat bugs,
thin bugs,
tiny-as-a-pin bugs.

Dark bugs,
bright bugs,
glowing little light bugs.

firefly

13

centipede

earwig

14

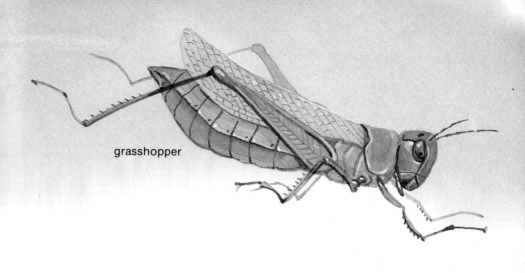

grasshopper

Bugs that scuttle,
bugs that creep,
bugs that wiggle,
jump, or leap.

click beetle

15

cicada

Bugs with feelers,
bugs with wings,
bugs that buzz
and bugs that sing.

16

monarch butterfly

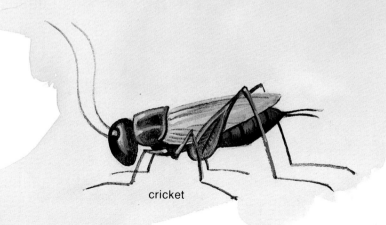

cricket

18

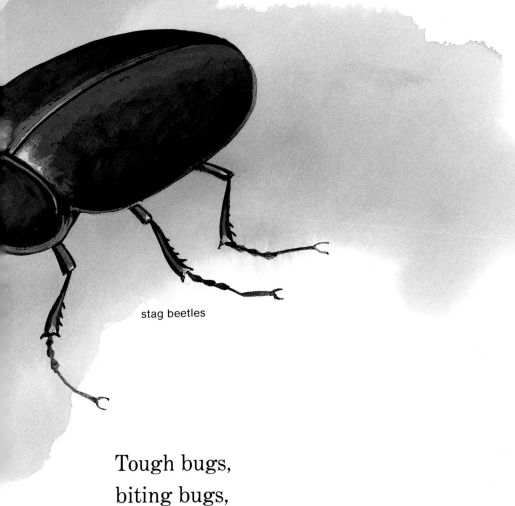

stag beetles

Tough bugs,
biting bugs,
sometimes even fighting bugs.

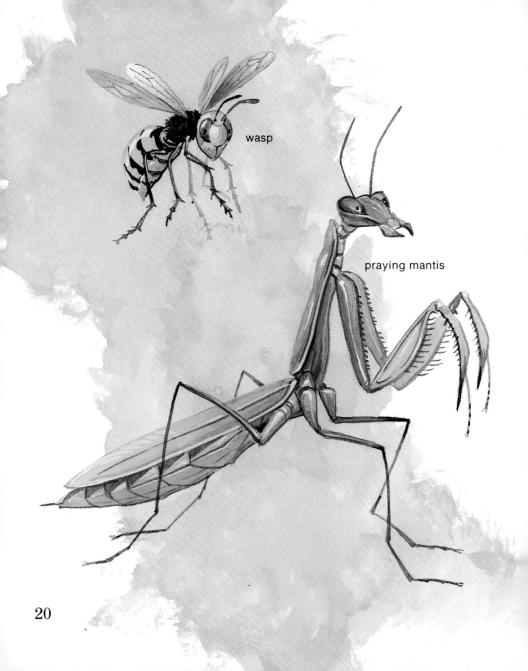

wasp

praying mantis

20

Mean bugs,
stinging bugs,
sticky little clinging bugs.

fleas

Bugs on dogs,
bugs in homes,

bugs who live
in honeycombs.

honeybee

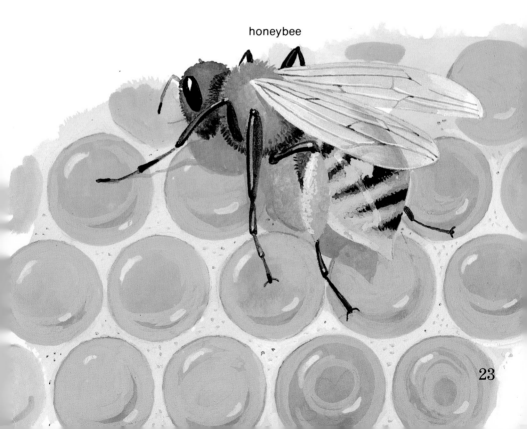

bumblebee

ant

Bugs in water,
bugs in clover,

water strider

24

bugs that make you itch
all over . . .

OUCH!

My jar's not full,
but now I see
that one smart bug
has hunted me!

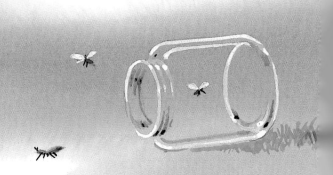

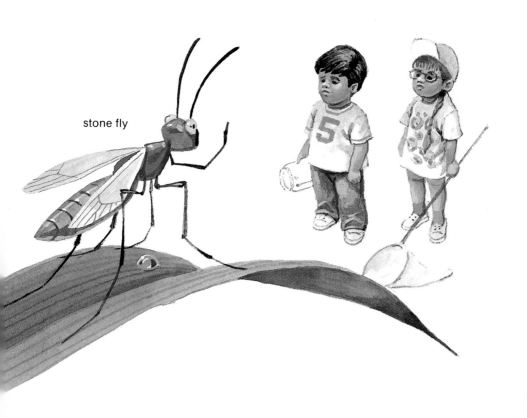

stone fly

I think he means-
Enough, my friend!
The Great Bug Hunt
is at an end!

30

WORD LIST

			means	stinging
a	dots	hunt	my	stripes
all	end	hunted	no	that
an	enough	I	not	the
and	even	in	now	thin
as	fat	is	on	think
at	feelers	itch	one	time
begins	fighting	jar	or	tiny
biting	find	jump	ouch	to
bright	fly	kinds	over	today
bug	friend	knows	pin	tough
bugs	full	leap	play	up
but	glowing	light	scuttle	water
buzz	grab	like	see	way
clinging	great	little	shapes	we
clover	has	live	sing	who
cobwebs	he	look	sizes	wiggle
crawl	high	make	smart	will
creep	homes	many	sometimes	wings
dark	honeycombs	me	spots	with
dogs	how	mean	sticky	you

About the Author

Bonnie Dobkin grew up with the last name Bierman in Morton Grove, Illinois. She attended Maine East High School and later received a degree in education from the University of Illinois. A high-school teacher for several years, Bonnie eventually moved into educational publishing and now works as an executive editor. She lives in Arlington Heights, Illinois.

For story ideas, Bonnie relies on her three sons, Bryan, Michael, and Kevin; her husband Jeff, a dentist; and Kelsey, a confused dog of extremely mixed heritage. When not writing, Bonnie focuses on her other interests—music, community theatre, and chocolate.

About the Artist

Tom Dunnington divides his time between book illustrations and wildlife painting. He has done many books for Childrens Press, as well as working on textbooks, and is a regular contributor to "Highlights for Children." Tom lives in Oak Park, Illinois.